Damn you Autocorrect! Best Of!
The best Autocorrect fails of all time

Copyright © 2013 by Gordon Sutherland

ISBN provided by
Cyprus Libary Registration of
Books and Serials

ISBN-13: 978-9963-2855-1-8
ISBN-10: 9-963-28551-1

Ebookboost Publishing ltd.

Give feedback on the book at:
facebook.com/BestOfAutocorrect

Auto correct makes you look pretty stupid sometimes. People texting a word but their phones auto correct feature suddenly has a mind of its own. So it´s Randomly correcting words incorrectly.

You like texting humor, or taking just a little bit of pleasure in the misfortune of others? This book brings together the best of Autocorrect fails. It is the full of funny and painfully embarrasing autocorrect fails. This book will leave you laughing until the end!

Message

DAMN YOU AUTOCORRECT BEST OF 2013

Waiting for prescription to be ready.

You are all you got it for
me is another Bengali you
all Landerset and many
more on the wall and her
mom and her mom I´ll
balance for my back and
you are gay

my phone made this
message for you. I´m not
crazy....

Maybe you´re not, but
your phone is! What was
that???

Message

DAMN YOU AUTOCORRECT BEST OF 2013

I´m such a narc! Kristina hates me, i´m sure. But us moms have to stick together, man. I fully expect you to eat my kid out.

Holy shit. That said rat!

Read the last sentence you wrote! lol

That´s so horrible.

Well i think they know its our job to rat them out!

I´m seriously crying laughing so hard.

Message

DAMN YOU AUTOCORRECT BEST OF 2013

What did you marinate it with?

paps blue ribbon beer and
secret spices and ranch ejaculation

extract!

not ejaculate!!!!!

That´s so funny!!!

Message

DAMN YOU AUTOCORRECT BEST OF 2013

They drained 10lbs of pussy fluid out if her abdomen

I mean : puss like fluid lol

omg sick and hilarious!

..ıll SERVICE 3G 4:20 PM

Message

DAMN YOU AUTOCORRECT BEST OF 2013

So what else is new man?

I start my new job with the
police force on Thursday

Just picked up my new
unicorn

You get your own unicorn?
Wow best job ever! Haha

I wouldn´t even be pissed
if i got pulled over by a
cop on a unicorn.

lol. You would be when
you saw the fine on the ticket.

10

Message

DAMN YOU AUTOCORRECT BEST OF 2013

Why is he staying?

Brodys family day or weekend or whatever

Ok... He can sleep in my bed if he wants.. Or naked since it is old bed... wash the sheets probly

Read your message mom!!!!!

Jakes! Not naked! Lol definately not naked lol

Omg!

Message

DAMN YOU AUTOCORRECT BEST OF 2013

Did you guys eat dinner yet?

Yep. Just had pasta...
Oh by the way, i laid the
babysitter.

Uh, excuse me?
You fucking what?

Haha Paid! I paid her.
Sorry to give you a heart
attack babe..

I hate you!

Lol!

Message

DAMN YOU AUTOCORRECT BEST OF 2013

Definitely! We talked about that this morning. And we have room for Dennis and Zoe too! I know Michelle wants to see all of you!

I have my air mistress that i can blow up and put in the office

Zoe and dennos can come uh Zoe have school so its gonna be just me

Shit... Matress not mistress!

I don´t own a blow up doll

Are you sure? Lol

Message

DAMN YOU AUTOCORRECT BEST OF 2013

Don´t worry, seriously.
He´s crazy about you and he
loves you so much.
He told me the other day that
you´re the first girl he
had ever thought about
the führer with.

What???????

Ok so that supposed
to say future...

Damn iPhone

Message

DAMN YOU AUTOCORRECT BEST OF 2013

I know. I´m terribly excited about it, let me tell ya.

I could fell the excitement jumping off your testicles!

Texts! I swearto god onerous texts!!!!

I wrote.. WTF

Stupid autocorrect!

My testicles are excited... too? lool

Message

DAMN YOU AUTOCORRECT BEST OF 2013

> What´s going on over there. Tom said you have ants?

Yes! It´s horrible. They´re in the kitchen and the dishwasher.

Mom´s been running around fingering everything in sight and it´s making the house smell so bad

> Now that´s a bad mental image. I´m scarred for life.

Fumigating, not fingering! Bad, autocorrect! BAD!

Message

DAMN YOU AUTOCORRECT BEST OF 2013

dude i´m so psyched for this weekend.

man on man, it´s gonna be epic!!

Man on man? You swing that way now?

MAN OH MAN! That was really bad!

Yes pretty much lol

Message

DAMN YOU AUTOCORRECT BEST OF 2013

Well I still see granny´s everywhere in their short skirts and high heels coming dangerously close to a ball slip.

TRANNYS

NOT GRANNY´S DEAR GOD

Hahahahaha! Grannies showing her balls again!

Hahahahaha auto correct is such a kidder :)

Message

DAMN YOU AUTOCORRECT BEST OF 2013

Yeah but the masturbate guy can´t get on the latter because it´s too windy out to fix it

Holly Shit. Maintenance guy.!!

I´m about to pee I´m laughing so hard

Oh crap I laughing so hard i just snorted and I´m going to have to re apply Eye makeup now

Hahahahaha! WIN!

Message

DAMN YOU AUTOCORRECT BEST OF 2013

> Going to be a bit late as nailing her sister. Please let her know for me.

You sure??

> Yeah why not? Just tell her please.

mum´s crying. She said you are being kicked out.

> Wtf? Oh my god, just read the text i sent. I meant MAILING. Thanks a bunch you fucking idiot! I´m ringing home right now!

Message

DAMN YOU AUTOCORRECT BEST OF 2013

Ohh. Poofy?

Yessssss

Yayyy :D

You´re having strippers at your nacho letter party.

Nacho letter.. omg

Omfg. Bachelorette party!!!

Omg I´m dying
Nacho letter Party!

Message

DAMN YOU AUTOCORRECT BEST OF 2013

I have an itchy lump on the
back of my head. Is it heroes?

Herpes

> I´ve heard thet heroes are
> born from head lumps of
> people with large heads.
> So don´t worry, it´s not
> herpes. Just hero fetus.

Should i shave that spot
so it can grow? Can i
abort it? I´m not sure I´m
ready for a hero

> You can´t deny the world a
> hero

Message

DAMN YOU AUTOCORRECT BEST OF 2013

Ohh even more fun!

Yes! What´re you doing my dear?

I´m playing cards with my dad again :)

Oooo bondage!

BONDING. BONDING. OMG BONDING.

O.M.G Worst Autocorrect ever!!!

Message

DAMN YOU AUTOCORRECT BEST OF 2013

Do you want chicken vaginas for dinner?

Excuse me

Omg fajitas

Wtf!

Sounds better than CHx vaginas

Still laughing

Srupid phone

Ahh stupid, I quit

Message

DAMN YOU AUTOCORRECT BEST OF 2013

> My dogs going crazy. I hate it when she is freaked out about something. it freaks me out!

Dude I know!

> She just sat on my dick and barfed for like 10 minutes at nothing. So creepy.

> Deck* barked* LOL

Bahahaha no your dick. XD

Still laughing

Message

DAMN YOU AUTOCORRECT BEST OF 2013

Grandma´s surgery went well! She is ok!

Great!!

Doctor says she could still develop a bloody clit.

Ew I thought the operation was on her elbow...

A blood clot!!!

My phone changes my words!

Get it together mom!

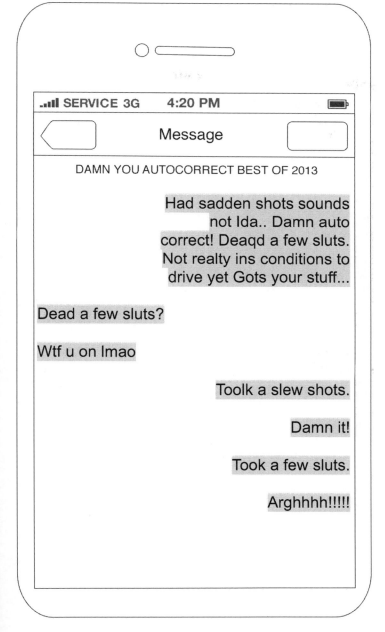

SERVICE 3G   4:20 PM

Message

DAMN YOU AUTOCORRECT BEST OF 2013

Had sadden shots sounds not Ida.. Damn auto correct! Deaqd a few sluts. Not realty ins conditions to drive yet Gots your stuff...

Dead a few sluts?

Wtf u on lmao

Toolk a slew shots.

Damn it!

Took a few sluts.

Arghhhh!!!!!

Message

DAMN YOU AUTOCORRECT BEST OF 2013

Ok I´m going to the goddamend post office today and mailing your brithday prawns.

Lol

Omg. Prawns! Lol!!
*Presents

I was all ewwww. Hahahah

Message

DAMN YOU AUTOCORRECT BEST OF 2013

ok lol

Have you sharted in my taxes yet?

Started!!! Please don´t shart on them :(

I have started and plan to finish Friday. Unless I shart of them.

Hahahahahahahhahah Lol

Message

DAMN YOU AUTOCORRECT BEST OF 2013

Hi daddy everything ok?

I just spent the last 3 hours in a bra

Soo yes everything is great!!!

In a bra? Does mom know? Lol

In a bar definitely not in a bra!

That´s a relief dad

Message

DAMN YOU AUTOCORRECT BEST OF 2013

What size battery does ur camera take? I have done new AA if any help? x

2x aa would be great

Cool I´ll pop them in my vag! x

Damn, bag not vag!!!!!! !!!!!!!!!!!!!!!!!!!!!!!!!!!!!!!!!!!

Pms!

Stupid auto erection!!

Auto correction! Bollox

Message

DAMN YOU AUTOCORRECT BEST OF 2013

oh yeah. It´s probably a 72 hour hold unless she chooses to stay longer, so maybe she´ll be out tonight.

Did you see Karen´s pussy? I don´t think she´s coming home tonight.

oh dude.... auto correct!!!

Post!! not pussy.. Ew.

Ahhhhaa!!!!!! my eyes!!!!! I can´t unsee that!!!

Lol

Message

DAMN YOU AUTOCORRECT BEST OF 2013

What time do you
finger yourself by??

OMG.. HAHAH

Grr figure you´ll be by,
damn auto correct!

Message

DAMN YOU AUTOCORRECT BEST OF 2013

YA! Haha it was STEEP!
:)

I bet!!!!

U still reading?

No? I´m watching legend
of korra with Jesse

Nice! Haha is he at your
house?

No we are at satans
apartment!

And by satan i mean
Sarah.... close enough.

Message

DAMN YOU AUTOCORRECT BEST OF 2013

Ireland is beautiful! You would really love it here.

I am so jealous!

Make sure you see the penis of man before you come home!

What!!! Lol mom are you drunk??? Penis of man..

Its not the kind of trip! Hahahah

Isle of man!!!!!!!! No PENIS!

Message

DAMN YOU AUTOCORRECT BEST OF 2013

Ah i see(: well good luck!
I hope you get it, it think I
am gonna get my breeding
license next summer right
after my 21st..

Breeding?? They should
require a license for that
these days. But i did´t
know you were thinking
about kids.

Lmao! Bartending.. Not
breeding Lmao Lmao
Lmao

Hahahah omg..

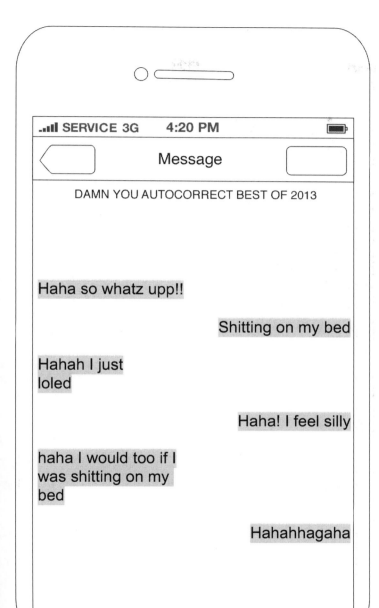

Message

DAMN YOU AUTOCORRECT BEST OF 2013

Haha so whatz upp!!

Shitting on my bed

Hahah I just loled

Haha! I feel silly

haha I would too if I was shitting on my bed

Hahahhagaha

Message

DAMN YOU AUTOCORRECT BEST OF 2013

This morning is ridiculous I just want to lick myself in the closet. I need 20 minutes for myself

Um. Lock. Not lick. But that was funny!

Speechless.. omg

Hahahah omg..

Message

DAMN YOU AUTOCORRECT BEST OF 2013

are you still at the walmart?

Yes why?

Ohh Good! I need more OPI nail polish.

The color name is NIPPLE PINK.

Hahahah seriously?

Omg NO! Tickled Pink! Hahahahahah

This phone... :(

Message

DAMN YOU AUTOCORRECT BEST OF 2013

American stuffers!!!!! I
am so disturbed.

I missed it !! what channel
does it come on?

Anal planet.
uh.....

i want to be totally
traumatized too!!

Omg! I think I am.

Animal

Lol

Message

DAMN YOU AUTOCORRECT BEST OF 2013

OK good. I washed ur
clitoris finally, ima bring
em to u when I get back

Woo CLOTHES!!!!!!!!!

....

That´s embarrassing..
llol

You washed my clitoris?
How nice of you! A true
friend!

F*** you auto correct!

Message

DAMN YOU AUTOCORRECT BEST OF 2013

I´m looking forward to the day
when I´m not blowing
minors every day.

Uhhhhh
Blowing minors?

My nose !!! Omg! Lmao!

I´m sick :(

DAMN YOU AUTOCORRECT BEST OF 2013

> No worries! I´ll send you good luck vibes

Thank u. I´ll need it. I´m nervous. I know it will be fine, but it blows.

> Lady- everything will work out. Ifeel it in my boner.

> Oh my god. My iPhone corrected bones to boner... I meant bones!!!!

Thatt was even better! Hahaha. Oh damn. Ur so great! xoxo

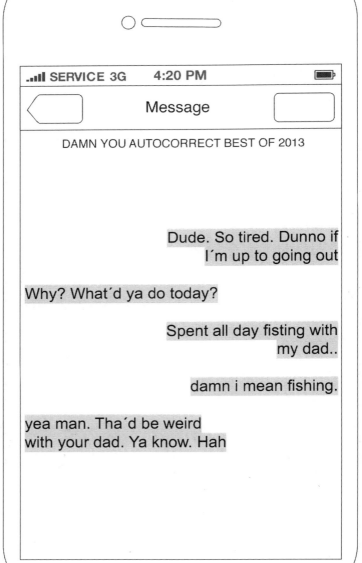

DAMN YOU AUTOCORRECT BEST OF 2013

Dude. So tired. Dunno if I´m up to going out

Why? What´d ya do today?

Spent all day fisting with my dad..

damn i mean fishing.

yea man. Tha´d be weird with your dad. Ya know. Hah

Message

DAMN YOU AUTOCORRECT BEST OF 2013

On the bike now. Done with weights. Ran into a friend. Talked to him for awhile.

Okay, I'm pooping in the shower.

What?

Omg Hahahha!!! Hopping! Wtf ! iPhone!! Lol!

I can't stop laughing

Thank god. That freaked me out!

Message

DAMN YOU AUTOCORRECT BEST OF 2013

Ok. how was golf?

Not bad

Course look nice?

Intercourse was great!

Lol damn you autocorrcet!

The "course" was great!

Lol. So I take it you found
the hole..lol

Message

DAMN YOU AUTOCORRECT BEST OF 2013

What are you wearing tonight?

A black penis skirt

Wait, what?

You´ll love the pattern :)

Omg Laughing too hard!!!

Message

DAMN YOU AUTOCORRECT BEST OF 2013

I bought you a couple thugs today for Valentines Day. I will ship them out to you Monday.

> Wow, isn´t that a bit overkill to keep the boys away from your little girl?

OMG!! I meant things. Lol

> Rofl

I am laughing so hard I have to cross my legs

> Lol don´t pee yourself Mommy

DAMN YOU AUTOCORRECT BEST OF 2013

You´re welcome.. do they have a drop box or should i bring them to the desk?

Yeah well the only Dropbox I know of is right on the front desk. They have a little slut.

Slut? Lol

Slot!!!!!!
They have a slot

:(

Hahah Sorry

Message

DAMN YOU AUTOCORRECT BEST OF 2013

Hey can you pick me up for work tomorrow? Car´s in the shop.

> Sure no prob. What´s wrong with the car?

I need new sluts.

> New Sluts? Impressive. I´d like to meet your mechanic lol.

Struts but if I could add sluts to my car I would.

> Truth.

Message

DAMN YOU AUTOCORRECT BEST OF 2013

What´s up?

> Not much. Just had to discipline my dog for peeing on the couch.

good for you! You show that dog your boobs!

OMG! I meant BOSS not boobs!

> Good. I was confused for a minute.

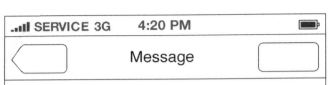

DAMN YOU AUTOCORRECT BEST OF 2013

I don´t want to talk about
this now.

> Whatever. I was not flirting
> with her.

Yeah that´s not what
Hannah said.

> She´s lying. I wish you
> would just breasfeed me.

> Believe , piece of crap!

Hahah OMG that is epic.
But I am still mad.

And I´m never going to
breastfeed you.

Message

DAMN YOU AUTOCORRECT BEST OF 2013

> What is your yearbook
> quote gonna be?

Oh it´s gona be based off
a Ralph Waldo Emerson
quote.

"*it´s not the journey but the
dusty kockitch that counts.*"

> Hahaha what!!! Jack that ist
> the worst qoute ever.

> I don´t thinkEmerson said
> that.. LMFAO

Destination WTF massive
fail..lol

Message

DAMN YOU AUTOCORRECT BEST OF 2013

I know this may sound dumb but is placenta considering a gluten? Was thinking of making that with chicken

For when you are here.

Placenta?!!! Like from a human?!!! Wtf?

:(((((

OMG! Stupid spell check. Polenta!

Can't stop giggling.

Message

DAMN YOU AUTOCORRECT BEST OF 2013

Hey Simon, pretty sure I put something in my burn I shouldn´t have! Is there Ny way to stop the cleaners emptying my bin?!? Sorry to bother you! x

Have you been drinking?

No not a drop!

Did you read the text you sent me ?

Oh my gosh .. the worst autocorrect ever!! Horric! Laughing!!

Message

DAMN YOU AUTOCORRECT BEST OF 2013

I know this may sound dumb but is placenta considering a gluten? Was thinking of making that with chicken

For when you are here.

> Placenta?!!! Like from a human?!!! Wtf?

> :(((((

OMG! Stupid spell check. Polenta!

Can´t stop giggling.

Message

DAMN YOU AUTOCORRECT BEST OF 2013

What does Sam need for his birthday besides that shirt?

Darth badger sleep pillow for his bed?

I have no idea what that is.

Just looks like his helmet as a fuzzy pillow.

Dude. Reread.

Now I´m crying in target.

I´m crying in the kitchen

Darth badger don´t care.

Message

DAMN YOU AUTOCORRECT BEST OF 2013

Did y´all enjoy dognuts

NO!

That is nasty.

The doughnuts were good though.

DAMN YOU AUTOCORRECT BEST OF 2013

Alright. I´m Hispanic.

...ur joking right? That´s what you wanted to tell me?

Emily this is kind of a big deal. I need your support!

Ok... Im sorry ur Hispanic??

What? OMG Just read the text...

I´m Homosexual, you know gay!

Lol autocorrect fail!

Wait.. what???????

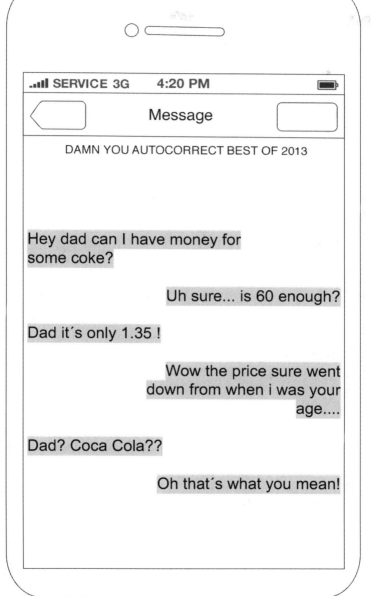

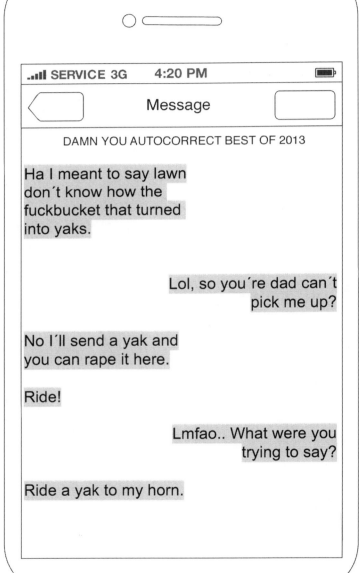

Message

DAMN YOU AUTOCORRECT BEST OF 2013

Can we set up a phone call for this afternoon?

Today isn´t good. I´ll be in and out of cunt all day. Tomorrow will be better.

Autocorrect. I meant court. I´m sencerely sorry.

Well this is awkward. I´ll be in touch tomorrow then. Thank you

Message

DAMN YOU AUTOCORRECT BEST OF 2013

wanna come over for
lunch?

No thanks. I´m so full. I
just ate 2 foot long hot
dongs.

oh i bet you just gobbled
those right up.

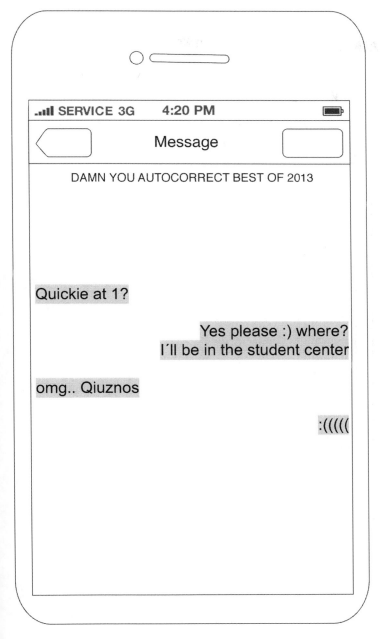

DAMN YOU AUTOCORRECT BEST OF 2013

Quickie at 1?

Yes please :) where?
I´ll be in the student center

omg.. Qiuznos

:(((((

DAMN YOU AUTOCORRECT BEST OF 2013

Are u alive I haven´t heard from you in like 24 hours

Yoo! I´m sorry I´m in the city with paul. Getting boned

Bombed!!!! hahah

Hahahahahah I wanna post that one one of those websites!

Loling

Message

DAMN YOU AUTOCORRECT BEST OF 2013

Are u alive I haven´t heard from you in like 24 hours

Yoo! I´m sorry I´m in the city with paul. Getting boned

Bombed!!!! hahah

Hahahahahah I wanna post that one one of those websites!

Loling

Message

DAMN YOU AUTOCORRECT BEST OF 2013

How did you make out with all that rain last night?

horrible! I have Waldo in my basement.

So that´s where he went. I´ve been looking for him for years! Haha

LMFAO *Water Stupid Autocorrect

Message

DAMN YOU AUTOCORRECT BEST OF 2013

Haha you sent your stuff to lightening 100 before?

I did on my last album.

Nothing.

Analbumcover.

Anal bum cover

An album cover

lol

Hahhahaha !

Message

DAMN YOU AUTOCORRECT BEST OF 2013

> They´ll usually bring in a closer in the 8th

> So that´s probably why

No i think Gandalf is still pitching.

I mean Felix

> Hahaha Gandalf

YOU SHALL NOT PASS!

Message

DAMN YOU AUTOCORRECT BEST OF 2013

So god was supposedly rescurrected on Easter?

Yes

So what is good Friday?

It is the day He died for your SYMPHONYBAR

Haha wow thanks! I Love chocolate. Praise him!

I wrote sins but you know what is funny. I write Symphonybar in my grocery list all the time.

Message

DAMN YOU AUTOCORRECT BEST OF 2013

Apparently, wood log thingies are not as ras as we thought. At least not at The Deathstar.

What´s Death Star?

Wal-Mart! Lol

Close enough! Lol

DAMN YOU AUTOCORRECT BEST OF 2013

You ok hon? You seem tired.

Yeah, I am. Rough day at work.

Spent the entire afternoon with a tranny.

Um, I can see how that might be tiring?

Hahah damn it to hell! I meant a trainee. And a dumb one.

Message

DAMN YOU AUTOCORRECT BEST OF 2013

Hey can you get pregnant before you come over today?

Whatt???

Oh my god. I meant to ask if you could get ptingles at the grocery store.

pringles .. the chips... NOT pregnant... gahaha

looool

Message

DAMN YOU AUTOCORRECT BEST OF 2013

> Utah? U are moving to Utah? Seriously?

Lol yeah

mostly because of the weather. It´s just so much easier to do crossdressing there.

> What! Have you lost your mind?

Lol Yeah i meant cross country. I´m increasing my training.

gonna call you

Message

DAMN YOU AUTOCORRECT BEST OF 2013

I didn´t even get those msgs lol. It was a parking ticket for parking on your moms ass. Mad me so mad

Wait no. Auto correct!

My moms ass!!! Bradddddd!! Hahahahaha

I´m sorry. That was a terrible autocorrect! If I parked there I prob would habe gotten a big ticket and arrested.

Message

DAMN YOU AUTOCORRECT BEST OF 2013

Eating cock puffs!

Cock puffs?

Hahahahahhahahaha hahahahahhaha

OMG! I mean coco puffs!!!!! Coco puffs!! Autocorrect!!!

Hahahahaha

That´s terrible I wonder how those would taste? Hahaha

Like chicken? :(

Message

DAMN YOU AUTOCORRECT BEST OF 2013

How are your classes this semester? Hard?

Yes. Very hard so far.

So I´ve been hitting the bong really hard.

I hit the bong really hard in college too. But it was the 70s.

I won´t tell you mother.

OMG - I meant books! Hahahah that was so funny.

Sure you did :)

Message

DAMN YOU AUTOCORRECT BEST OF 2013

So what´s the deal?

I can´t come. My mom won´t let me borrow her vibrator.

Ooomgggg

That might be the funniest thing I´ve ever read

HAHAHA she won´t let me borrow her vibe

As is in crappy Pontiac

Lol i know what a vibe is. And I´m dying.

Message

DAMN YOU AUTOCORRECT BEST OF 2013

I got paid to watch movies, eat pizza, and sleep. Best babysitting job ever.

I´ve gotten those before. I lube the kids when they´re asleep!

You. What.

OHMYGAWD NO. I´m not a pedo. I tried to say I love the kids when they´re asleep.

I´m laughing os hard right now.

Message

DAMN YOU AUTOCORRECT BEST OF 2013

Close enough

Little blonde haired bullshit babies :)

BLUE EYED not bullshit

> Little bullshit babies...Can we have at least one baby that's not full of shit?

I have my very own damn u autocorrect now!!

Message

DAMN YOU AUTOCORRECT BEST OF 2013

I´m thrusting right now and it´s actually really fun. Can you believe it?

What does that mean?

Oh my god I meant THRIFTING like in a thrift store.

Omg, my mind was going wild places :o

I can imagine...

Message

DAMN YOU AUTOCORRECT BEST OF 2013

Did you leave yet? Hurry up!!!!

Coming. Just fingering this last doll.

Youre what???

Yikes I meant finishing! So embarrassed. Leaving now!

Message

DAMN YOU AUTOCORRECT BEST OF 2013

> I hope the directions to the hospital arrive before the baby dies. :)

Jesus Christ, I´m not sure where that cam from

> Does!!! OMG DOES! Fucking autocorrect did that! I hope you know I´d never say something like that.

I´m not going to mention this to Jill.

DAMN YOU AUTOCORRECT BEST OF 2013

Just when I thought I ran out, I found a full box of condoms in my room!!

Uh Maddie you have never even had a bf why do you need those?

CONTACTS CONTACTS For my eyes! AUTO CORRECT

You had to point out my love life? Duck you!

SERVICE 3G   4:20 PM

Message

DAMN YOU AUTOCORRECT BEST OF 2013

No freaking clue what to get mom for christmas.

Yea I know

Just run into Hallmark and grab her a horny man.

Oh they sell those there now? Good to know next time I´m in a pinch.

WTF how does ornament become horny man!!! Lmao I am laughing so had.

I´m sure mom would appreciate a horny man.

Message

DAMN YOU AUTOCORRECT BEST OF 2013

I have a sinus infection

what about the bad cough?

I know they gave me antibiotics for my cold and liquid codeine to suppress my cock

Ok hopefully you will be better soon. R u getting meds now?

Hahahahha omg auto correct!!

Message

DAMN YOU AUTOCORRECT BEST OF 2013

I watched the trailer and it looks good.

Yah definitely. I´ve never seen it actually.

I brought some porn home to toss in my salad if you want some

Mmmm. Sounds like a good salad lol

**PORK!

That´s an epic spell check

Message

DAMN YOU AUTOCORRECT BEST OF 2013

Ok, message men later
and let me who you
are doing, love you!

Hahaha best
combination of typos ever!

DAMN YOU AUTOCORRECT BEST OF 2013

I have someone elses
come on me ew ew ew ew

Is it devins if its his its ok
if it´s not i will kill you

No i don´t know who´s it is
its attached to my shirt
and pocket book I think it
was on the seat :(

.......please tell me this was
supposed to say gum...

Omg yes.. that´s awkward..
GUM!

I´m dying! Xd

DAMN YOU AUTOCORRECT BEST OF 2013

And if this doesn´t work
don´t worry about it. We
will make it work later.

Come tomorrow. And that
way we can spread out the
thrusting goodness.

Lol. Read that to your self.

Looool . Fuuudge.

I menat thrifting

Message

DAMN YOU AUTOCORRECT BEST OF 2013

Can I have a huge hug or are apple employes not allowed to sho erection?

Affection!!!!

I´m literally laughing.

Hahaha I am so so sorry!

FAIL!!

Message

DAMN YOU AUTOCORRECT BEST OF 2013

We can eat anywhere arround Fremont or back here in San Jose like Dave and busters.

> K whatever sounds good to you.

> So i will be the disgusted driver.

> Hahaha DESIGNATED driver. Damn autocorrect!

Message

DAMN YOU AUTOCORRECT BEST OF 2013

We need orgasms

disregard. That last
message was : We need
ORANGES! And it was
meant for my room mate.

> oh for a second there i was
> getting happy..lol

> but yes tell your roomate
> to pick me up bag of orgasms
> while shes at the store too please!
> hahaha

So, that was about
oranges. I would much
rather have a bag or orgasms
than oranges

> would´t we all. lol

DAMN YOU AUTOCORRECT BEST OF 2013

Indeed. What are you up to?

I bought some slaves at Ikea today. Wanted to put em up.

........SHELVES!!!!

... :)

DAMN YOU AUTOCORRECT BEST OF 2013

I have my first date with Justin today! Going hiking.

Okay! Have fun!

Do yourself a favor: wear really thick makeup!

That was so mean

Wow... You have no reply? Okay then.

I meant mittens! It is 24 degrees.

Message

DAMN YOU AUTOCORRECT BEST OF 2013

OMG. Help! I´m obsessed
with sodomy!

Giving or receiving?

Oh my god .. oh my god!
I meant Sodoku!!

Shittttt!

LMAO!!

Message

DAMN YOU AUTOCORRECT BEST OF 2013

Let´s go to the beach tomorrow. I have the day off!!

> I can´t go till around 2. Getting my carped munched at 11.

And who is munching your carpet? Does John know? Hahahaha

> Ahhh!! I meant to say scrubbed.

> DAMN!!!

Message

DAMN YOU AUTOCORRECT BEST OF 2013

How's the move going?

Need any head?

Need and head? What do you mean?

F*** "Help" Do you need help! I was not offering you a sexual favor!

Hello?

Dude tell me you know what auto correct is.

Message

DAMN YOU AUTOCORRECT BEST OF 2013

I love it when you call me Bug Poppa..

Hahaha bug poppa?!

Damn autocorrect!

Message

DAMN YOU AUTOCORRECT BEST OF 2013

Have u been a good boy :)

yea. Except i may or may not have bought a lapdance last night.

A lapdance? Are you kidding me right now?

no wait!

No you wait, what kind of business trip are you on. I´m pissed aaron that is fucked up!

Married men don´t get lap dances

I meant laptop! Stupid Auto correct!!!

..ıll SERVICE 3G   4:20 PM

Message

DAMN YOU AUTOCORRECT BEST OF 2013

> Babe I don´t feel like cooking tonight. You bring home human beef?

WTF? I´m in a meeting. Human beef? Are you high?

> Hunan beef! The place that just opened on 7th ave!!

> I´m laughing so had I almost pucked.

Jesusu! I Just laughed out loud and could possibly get fire now. Order
your human beef. I´ll pick it up at 6. Love you

Message

DAMN YOU AUTOCORRECT BEST OF 2013

Our house for christmas this year. You are coming right?

Yea!

You cooking? Or Alison?

Me. I am gonna dry hump the roast 3 days before.

Okay that´s a bad visual. On second thought maybe I will stay home. Lol

Dry humping
Dry rub

Message

DAMN YOU AUTOCORRECT BEST OF 2013

What did you guys do on day two of your vacation?

Snoggled on clit bags.

Uhhh...

Snoggled on light boys.

Dad are you drunk?

I´m trying to say we snorkeled on little bay!!!

Ohh! How was the snorkeling?

DAMN YOU AUTOCORRECT BEST OF 2013

Oh i was going to ask do you know anyone who has a rocket tickler that i can borrow for a hole..

Holy shit! NOOO

That's not what I meant at all!!!

Let me try again

> Lmao!! I can hardly text I am laughing so hard.

A roto tiller that i can borrow for a while! Wow really iPhone! Oh my god

Message

DAMN YOU AUTOCORRECT BEST OF 2013

Are you still at Lisa´s house?

> Yes and I just got her pussy slobber all over my jeans

Ewwwwwww what?

> OMG her puppys slobber.

> That sounded so bad!

I was confused!

Message

DAMN YOU AUTOCORRECT BEST OF 2013

> Wanna go get ice cream with me and jenni?

hell to yes

> Cool! Is your brother gonna come? Jenni asked

no. he is asshole intolerant.

> Are you saying we are assholes? Thats mean!

no i meant lactose intolerant! Automobile correct.

see?

DAMN YOU AUTOCORRECT BEST OF 2013

Hey fag I got the pkg
last night! Thank you!

> Fag? That's a nice
> way to talk to your father.

Opppps! Dad!! Auto
correct! I swear!

Ohh god I hurt
from laughing!

> Me too my boyfriend
> and I are crying right
> now!

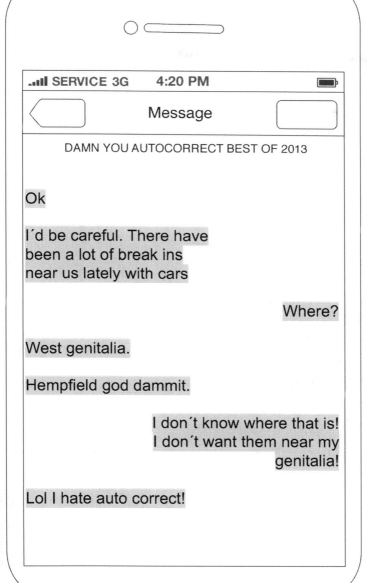

Message

DAMN YOU AUTOCORRECT BEST OF 2013

Ok

I´d be careful. There have been a lot of break ins near us lately with cars

Where?

West genitalia.

Hempfield god dammit.

I don´t know where that is! I don´t want them near my genitalia!

Lol I hate auto correct!

Message

DAMN YOU AUTOCORRECT BEST OF 2013

How the hell did you even get that Christmas tree in your house?

Your front door is tiny.

I had to take it up the butt.

son of a bitch.

Up the back. I thru the kitchen.

That sounds like a real "pain in the ass". haha

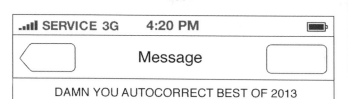

DAMN YOU AUTOCORRECT BEST OF 2013

At starbuck. Want anything?

Ohooo yes. Please bring me back a tall white hot chic.

Sorry, no hot white chics here but there´s a Latina in the corner whose kinda cute.

HOT Choc!! I swear my phone wants me to be a lesbian so bad.

Just give in! Do not resist!

Message

DAMN YOU AUTOCORRECT BEST OF 2013

Cuz I knew your bday was coming up soon silly. i´m not inseminating anything else

****Insunuating*****
I apologize so many levels.

OMG OMG OMG
I literally have no words.
But a birthday card will be
just fine.. no insemination
necessary.

‹ Message ☐

DAMN YOU AUTOCORRECT BEST OF 2013

Did you leave yet?

No, I´m still downstairs fondling the landlady.

I am fondling the landlady!

Quake happening again.

What?

Fondling the laundry

Fondling the landlady downstairs in an earthqauke. Ok got it.

This was a great chat.

Message

DAMN YOU AUTOCORRECT BEST OF 2013

Are we doing toyys for tots at the restaurant this year?

Yes! We´re giving a free appetizer if you bring tits.

I mean, free app if you bring a wrapped toy for the cyclops.

Tits

Best promotion ever mom!

I am calling you F*** this.

Message

DAMN YOU AUTOCORRECT BEST OF 2013

> Josh cracks his knuckles and it drives me mental.

Oh I feel you. JT does that too.

And he constantly eats off my platypus. So damned annoying.

> I can see how that might be troubling.

Lol wut??? Plate. I don´t have my own platypus. But i wish I did.

> Hahah it would make game night much more interesting.

Message

DAMN YOU AUTOCORRECT BEST OF 2013

Is it just a imagination or is the black wieder bigger than the white one?

Wait.. waht are we talking about? Lmao.

Damn It! The Wii. Isn´t the black wii bigger than the white one.

Just made my day.

Message

DAMN YOU AUTOCORRECT BEST OF 2013

Want me to come over .)

no - my parents are homelese

*home
stupid autocorrect!

119

Message

DAMN YOU AUTOCORRECT BEST OF 2013

You mean you´re not going to hand stich a blanket and baby clothes?

I was going to make a blanket with my man hai but i thought that would be taking things to far.

Ew thats disgusting...

Bare hands!!! Not man hair!

Message

DAMN YOU AUTOCORRECT BEST OF 2013

Woooho So glad...
Mike stank up my cooch!

My chouch!! COUCH!!
Ducking autocorrect...

Lol. I am sure he has done
his fair share of stinking up
your chooch

Lol no My Cooch always
smells temting...

Message

DAMN YOU AUTOCORRECT BEST OF 2013

What you guys up to tonight?

Dinner, and the taking the kids to see pussy 'n butts

You taking your child to a strip club? Hahah. Mother of the year!

Ha! I meant we´re seeing pus in butts

Pussy in boots

Puss in boots?

Ahhh yes!

DAMN YOU AUTOCORRECT BEST OF 2013

Great news!!! I finally found my gspot.

Um wow. Thank you so much for sharing. Congratulations?

I found it in the back seat of my car.

Ok mom now this is just getting too weird. I know we are close but come on.

Huh?

Og god! My GPS! Hahahahaha!!

13418189R00070

Printed in Great Britain
by Amazon.co.uk, Ltd.,
Marston Gate.